Quality 17.56

408075
796.355
Con

W9-AAY-484

DISCARD

408075

SPORTS FROM COAST TO COAST™

FIELD HOCKEY

RULES, TIPS, STRATEGY, AND SAFETY

— HELEN CONNOLLY ———

rosen central™

The Rosen Publishing Group, Inc.,
New York

SHELBYVILLE-SHELBY COUNTY
PUBLIC LIBRARY

Published in 2005 by The Rosen Publishing Group, Inc.
29 East 21st Street, New York, NY 10010

Copyright © 2005 by The Rosen Publishing Group, Inc.

First Edition

All rights reserved. No part of this book may be reproduced in any form without permission in writing from the publisher, except by a reviewer.

Library of Congress Cataloging-in-Publication Data

Connolly, Helen.
Field hockey: rules, tips, strategy, and safety / Helen Connolly.—1st ed.
    v. cm.—(Sports from coast to coast)
Includes bibliographical references and index.
Contents: The history of field hockey—What's needed to play the game—
Playing the game—Offense, defense, and the future of field hockey.
ISBN 1-4042-0182-3 (library binding) 1. Field hockey—Juvenile literature.
[1. Field hockey.] I. Title. II. Series.
GV1017.H7E43 2004
796.355—dc22
                                                          2003022266

Manufactured in the United States of America

CONTENTS

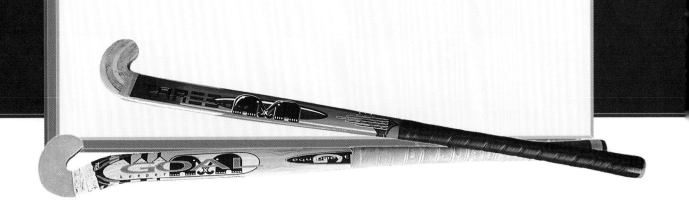

CHAPTER ONE

The History of Field Hockey

This Greek carving (*top*) from around 500 BC and this medieval calendar from AD 1450 (*bottom*) are among the earliest images of field hockey.

Field hockey is the oldest known ball-and-stick game. No one is certain exactly where or when the game was invented, but there is evidence that the game existed in ancient times. Four-thousand-year-old drawings of men playing a form of field hockey were found in a tomb in Egypt. Over the centuries, different versions of the sport were played by the Arabs, Aztecs, Ethiopians, Greeks, Persians, and Romans. Field hockey is connected to other established games like Germany's *kolbe* and the French game *hocquet*, from which sport historians believe the term "hockey" was derived. But it was in England in the mid-1800s that field hockey evolved into the sport we know today.

The first men's hockey club, Blackheath, was formed in southeast London in 1849. A field hockey club is like a league with several teams and is organized by region. However, it was another hockey club in London, Teddington, that helped refine and modernize the game. Teddington developed certain conventions, such as the use of the striking circle, the area of the field that a player must be in to score a goal, and the banning of lifting sticks above the shoulder. Thirty-seven years later, in 1886, the Hockey Association was founded in London.

While men's field hockey clubs were gaining in popularity, the heavy ball and thick sticks that were used could potentially hurt a person, so in those times the game was considered too dangerous for women to play. However, as leisure activities like croquet, another ball-and-stick sport, became socially acceptable for women to play, the equipment used in field hockey didn't seem as threatening. Physical activity was difficult for women in the Victorian era because of the heavy layers of clothing and ankle-length dresses they were expected to wear. It was difficult to move, let alone run, in such apparel. In spite of that, women did take up the sport. In fact, today most women's field hockey uniforms include a kilt, making field

The Shape of the Ball

The Blackheath field hockey club played with a solid cube of black rubber for the "ball." Teddington eventually introduced the use of a spherical ball.

hockey one of the few sports in which women wear a skirt on the field. As more and more women became involved in field hockey, it was eventually deemed a team sport that was proper for women to play, the first one of its kind. In 1887, the first women's hockey club was created in East Mosley in northern England. Two years later, the All England Women's Hockey Association was founded.

As field hockey became a favorite pastime among both sexes in England, its popularity began to spread around the world. The British army introduced the game in the late 1800s to India. This subsequently led to the first international competition in 1895. In 1908, men's field hockey had been approved as an Olympic sport and was played at the Olympic Games in London that same year.

Eventually, field hockey spread to the United States, pretty much as a result of the efforts of a twenty-eight-year-old English woman named Constance Applebee. In the summer of 1901, Applebee, a physical education teacher, was attending a seminar at Harvard University in Massachusetts. She was alarmed and horrified by the lack of exercise she observed in young American women, so she put together an impromptu hockey exhibition behind the Harvard gymnasium. Because of the enthusiastic response to the game at Harvard,

Applebee began to travel around to the most prestigious women's colleges in the Northeast, starting up field hockey teams at Vassar, Wellesely, Smith, Radcliffe, Mount Holyoke, and Bryn Mawr. Later that same year, the American Field Hockey Association, an organization for women players, was founded in Philadelphia, and Constance Applebee was elected president.

The Victorian era imposed a lot of restrictions on women in terms of clothing, behavior, and lifestyle. Women were expected to obey men, and any outspokenness, playfulness, or athletic activity that went beyond parlor games was strongly discouraged. By the turn of the century, however, women began to agitate for equality in politics, in the workplace, and in social relations. When Constance Applebee arrived in America in 1901 to teach young female college students the game of field hockey, the suffrage movement was in full swing. Women wanted the same basic rights as men to develop mentally and physically as individuals. Increased enrollment in women's colleges and interest in field hockey reflected these desires. Because of Applebee's efforts during field hockey's early stages in America, it became known mostly as a women's sport in the United States.

In 1920, a U.S. women's touring team began to compete internationally. Three years later, Constance Applebee opened the first field hockey camp, Tegawitha Hockey Camp, in the Pocono Mountains in Pennsylvania. Girls went to Tegawitha to increase their skills and to meet other women who enjoyed the game. They exercised and ran practice drills by day and studied the theory of the sport by night. The camp remained successful for decades and eventually grew to encompass a variety of athletic activities for women, until the camp closed

at the end of the twentieth century. Applebee continued to play an important role in pioneering this burgeoning competitive sport for women in the United States until she retired in 1971, at the age of 97. After her retirement, Applebee moved back to England, where she lived until her death at the age of 107!

In the United States, men's field hockey never really caught on in the way that women's field hockey did, but men do play it. The first recorded men's game wasn't played until 1928 in Pennsylvania. Later that year, the Field Hockey Association of America (FHAA), an organization for men's field hockey, was founded. In 1930, the FHAA became a member of the Fédération Internationale de Hockey (FIH), hockey's international federation. An American named Henry Greer, who many consider the founder of men's hockey in the United States, was president of the FHAA from 1930 to 1959. Greer coached and played on the U.S. men's team in its first Olympic Games in Los Angeles in 1932. It took home the bronze medal that year, losing to Japan, who took the silver, and India, who took the gold.

Although the sport had been played by women since its inception, women's field hockey didn't receive recognition for serious international competition until the 1970s, when, in 1975, the first Women's World Cup was held. Women's field hockey wasn't added to the Olympic program until 1980. That year, the Olympics were held in Moscow in what was then the Soviet Union. Because of the political climate at the time, the United States was not on friendly terms with

Constance Applebee introduced field hockey to the women of Harvard University in 1901. Field hockey became popular quickly, and it wasn't long before the United States Field Hockey Association (USFHA) was formed.

A player from the United States eludes three defenders from the Australian team during the 1984 Olympics. Field hockey has become an international phenomenon, and dozens of teams represent their countries in Olympic competitions.

the Russians. Along with sixty-one other countries, the Americans decided to boycott the 1980 games. It wasn't until the 1984 Olympic Games in Los Angeles that the women's field hockey team actually got to compete. It took home the bronze medal that year.

The United States Olympic Committee (USOC) urged the FHAA and the United States Field Hockey Association (USFHA) to merge, and in 1993, they formed one national organization for both women's and men's field hockey, retaining the name of USFHA. The USFHA is an active organization today, with 15,000 members. It is a member of the USOC, the Pan American Hockey Federation (PAFH), and the FIH. The USFHA continues to promote the sport of field hockey and to prepare teams to participate in international games, including the Olympics.

Today, field hockey is enjoyed by millions of men and women in nearly ninety countries. Its popularity continues to grow, with new clubs and teams, both amateur and professional, sprouting up all over. It is acknowledged as one of the largest team sports in the world, second only to soccer.

CHAPTER TWO

Equipment Needed

Like cricket players, field hockey players wear pads for protection. At one time, field hockey players used a cricket ball for competition.

As field hockey was gaining momentum in the late 1800s in England, cricket, another ball-and-stick game, somewhat similar to American baseball, had already been embraced as an English pastime. At first, it was natural for field hockey enthusiasts to use leather-covered cricket balls, but today the field hockey ball is very different. It is completely constructed out of polyvinyl chloride (PVC), which is a type of hard plastic. The plastic ball proved to be better for outdoor games, as it will not absorb any moisture. It is also built to withstand the heat of friction and the frequent impacts of bouncing. The ball is slightly larger than an American baseball, measuring about 9 inches (23 centimeters) in circumference and weighing about 5.5 ounces (156 grams). Younger players are permitted to play with a lighter ball. An official game ball is dimpled like a golf ball, but practice balls are not required to be. For international games, the ball color must be white, but for other games the ball can be any color, just so long as it contrasts with the color of the field for better visibility. When hit with the field hockey stick, the ball can reach speeds of up to 100 miles per hour (161 kilometers per hour).

Due to its weight, texture, and speed, a field hockey ball could potentially cause serious injury to a player if it makes contact with an unprotected area of the body. This is why players are required to wear shin guards and mouth guards. Hockey shin guards are made from lightweight plastic or foam and are crucial in protecting players' legs from speeding balls and heavy, swinging sticks. Because of the protection that shin guards provide, players have the confidence to play more aggressively, which in turn, improves their game.

When women's field hockey was founded in America, players were required to wear a modest and cumbersome ensemble that included long-sleeved flannel shirts and corduroy skirts that fell several inches below the knee. Thankfully, the modern-day women's field hockey uniforms, consisting of a short-sleeved shirt and a kilt, are much more comfortable. Many women wear shorts,

This Dartmouth College player takes warm-up shots before a game. Because field hockey is such a physically demanding sport, it is important for players to stay in good shape.

similar to bicycle shorts, under their kilts to protect their legs when diving for balls. Men's and children's field hockey uniforms are virtually the same, except that men wear shorts instead of kilts. Members of the same team are required to wear matching uniforms and the same color kneesocks. Shirts are required to have a number printed on the front and back so that the referees can identify each player.

Because of the amount of running involved in field hockey and the importance that is placed on quickness and agility, footwear with proper support is essential. For outdoor grass fields, leather or nylon cleats are needed for traction. For indoor games with a flat Astroturf field, flat-soled running shoes are suitable.

Both men and women goalkeepers wear shorts and a shirt that differ in color from that of their team and the opponent's team. Goalies are required to cover nearly their whole body with protective

Professional players can drive the ball faster than 100 miles per hour (161 km/h). As a result, field hockey goalies have to wear a lot of safety gear. Without this padding, a goalie risks serious injury.

The left glove of a goalkeeper has additional padding in the palm for blocking shots. The right glove is more flexible, for gripping the stick. The stick is held by the goalkeeper in the right hand only.

gear that will shield them from serious injury, while at the same time allowing for mobility. Field hockey goalies wear helmets with face masks, similar to those of ice hockey goalies. They also wear a throat guard, a chest pad, shoulder pads, elbow pads, an abdominal guard, padded overall pants with a pelvic guard, leg pads, large gloves with padded knuckles, and "kickers" for the feet and ankles. Kickers are lightweight boots that are worn over the shoes and are used to kick the ball out of the striking circle.

Aside from protective gear, the most important piece of equipment that a player owns is his or her stick. Field hockey sticks are used to handle the ball on the field. The sticks have a straight handle and shaft and a curved head. They are made of wood, are about 3 feet long (0.9 meters), and must weigh between 12 and 28 ounces (340 to 794 g). It is important for a player to take into account his or her own height and strength when picking a stick size that would best suit him or her and enhance performance on the field. A common way to choose the proper stick length is to place the head of the stick on the ground next to the leg. The handle of the stick should come up to the top of a player's hip. All sticks must be able to pass through

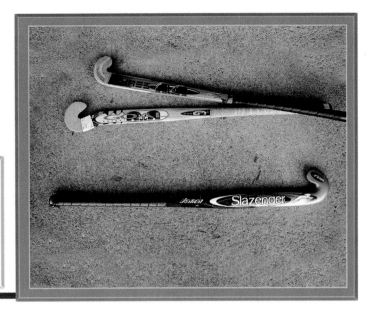

Field hockey sticks are different from ice hockey sticks. Originally made out of wood, field hockey sticks can now be made with high-tech synthetic materials.

a 2-inch (5.1 cm) ring, from the head to the handle. If a stick cannot pass through such a ring, it cannot be used in a game.

The ball can only be hit with the front, or flat half, of the stick. The design of the stick has changed over the years, but today the two most important features of a stick are its reinforcement and the shape of the head. The stiffer a field hockey stick, the harder it will hit the ball. Reinforcements are important in making the stick stronger and improving a player's game. There are some materials that can be added to a basic wooden shaft and handle in order to make it stronger. Fiberglass will add strength and will lengthen the life span of a stick. Both Kevlar and Dyneema will increase shock absorbency while carbon will add stiffness. A player will strive to pick a stick made of materials that will do the most to complement his or her particular skills or style of playing.

The curved head of the stick cannot be made of any material other than wood, and it cannot be larger than 4 inches (10 cm), no matter the size of the player. Sharp edges are not permitted. Instead, the edges must be completely rounded. The three main head shapes are the shorti, the midi, and the hook. The shorti is the traditional

Different sticks have different strengths and weaknesses. The kind of stick a player uses depends on his or her style and position.

head shape and is preferred by many players for the extra dexterity it affords. Because shorti heads are carved from one piece of wood, they are stronger and longer lasting, and they have a more centered "sweet spot" for striking. Midi and hook heads are made of several pieces of wood that are laminated together. They aren't as strong or durable as shorti heads, but as long as a player takes proper care of his or her stick, midi and hook heads can be used for a considerable amount of time. Midi and hook heads are advantageous for dribbling and flicking (when a player snaps his or her wrist to lift the ball in the air for quick passes or shots).

The shafts of the sticks can also come in different shapes. While straight shafts are more common, some players, particularly goalies, prefer a kinked shaft. When laid on its side, a kinked shaft can stop a ball better than a straight stick, offering a goalie a larger save area.

After a player has chosen the proper stick to optimize his or her game, he or she needs to learn how to hold the stick properly. When someone picks up a field hockey stick for the first time, his or her first instinct might be to hold it like one would hold a baseball bat. However, the proper way to hold a stick is called the "shake hands grip." It is achieved by reaching out the left hand as if to shake someone's hand and grabbing the top of the handle of the stick, so the flat side is aligned with the palm of the left hand. The second step is to reach out with the right hand, as if to shake someone's hand, placing the right hand about 5 to 7 inches (13 to 18 cm) below the left hand.

The head of the stick should point forward and slightly to the right, with the toe pointing up and the flat side of the stick facing to the left. It should be held comfortably away from the player's body. The left hand controls the stick's movement, while the right hand serves as a guide.

Because the ball can only be hit with the flat side of the stick, it must be hit a different way when the ball is on the player's left side. The "reverse grip" is used for this purpose. It is achieved by loosening the grip of the right hand and turning the left hand until the inside of the left wrist is facing up. The flat side faces to the right with the toe pointing toward the player. Once the transition is made from shake hands to reverse grip, the right-hand grip should tighten. It is important for a player to retain a firm grip on the stick with his or her fingers together. When the player's fingers become separated, there is a greater chance for injury caused by stray sticks and balls.

CHAPTER THREE

Playing the Game

Field hockey is a fun sport for people of all ages to play.

Once a player has the essential equipment, the actual fun and excitement of playing the game on the field can begin. Field hockey is often played outdoors on the grass, but more serious competitions take place indoors on a completely flat Astroturf surface, where the players and the ball can move faster. Whether the game is played indoors or out, the size and markings of the field remain the same.

The standard size of a field hockey field is rectangular, measuring 60 yards (55 m) wide by 100 yards (91 m) long. The field is divided into two halves by the centerline. Each half of the field is then divided by a 25-yard (23 m) line. All lines on the field must be 3 inches (7.6 cm) wide. The end line, the goal line (the part of the end line between the goal posts), and the sidelines are all part of the field of play. This means that in order for a ball to be out of bounds or for a goal to be scored, the ball must completely pass over any of those lines.

In each corner of the field, a flag is placed at the outer edge of the line. A flag is also placed at each 25-yard (23 m) line, 1 yard (0.9 m) outside the sidelines. The flags assist the referee on where to award a free hit to the offense when the defense commits a foul within its 25-yard (23 m) area. There are six lines, measuring 2 yards (1.8 m) in length, that are placed across the centerline and 5 yards (4.6 m) away from and parallel to each sideline. The purpose of these lines is to assist in determining where sideline hits should be taken after a ball is knocked out of bounds. Twelve-inch-long (30 cm) lines are placed 16 yards (15 m) away from and parallel to the end line. Other 12-inch (30 cm) lines, penalty corner hit marks, are placed inside the field on the end lines at 5- and 10-yard (4.6 and 9.1 m) intervals, measured from the sides of the goalposts. Finally, the penalty spot, where the ball is placed to take a penalty shot, is placed 7 yards (6.4 m) from the center of the goal line.

The shooting circle, or striking circle, is actually a semicircle. The ends are 16 yards (15 m) from each goal post, creating an area that

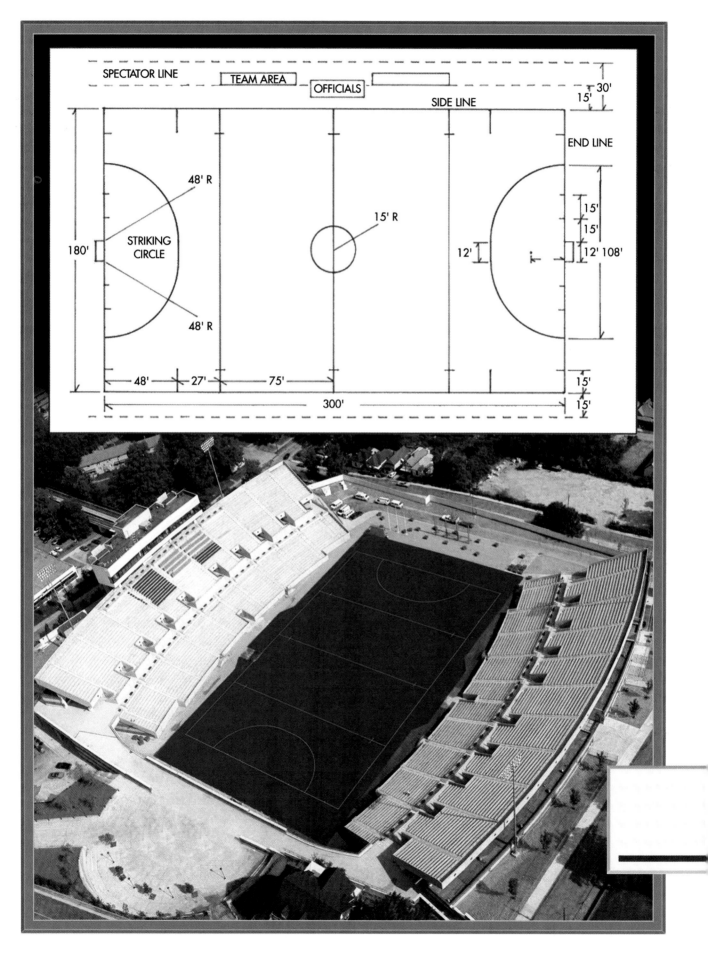

extends 16 yards (15 m) into the field, with a 4-yard (3.7 m) straight line parallel to the goal line. The object of the game is to shoot the ball in the opponent's goal for one point. The team with the most points at the end of a game wins. A score can only be made by a shot taken from within the striking circle. The ball must pass completely over the goal line in order for a score to count. Additionally, the ball cannot be lifted or flicked into the circle, but must be brought or passed in on the ground.

At each end of the field is a goal cage constructed out of two goalposts, a horizontal crossbar, a backboard, and sideboards, with a net covering the top and sides. Like the field, the goal cage is rectangular, measuring 12 feet wide (3.7 m) by 7 feet high (2.1 m). The posts and crossbar are painted white, while the backboard is painted dark and measures 18 inches (46 cm) high. The sideboards also measure 18 inches (46 cm) high and are 4 feet (1.2 m) wide, which determines the depth of the goal area.

Each team has a captain on the field at all times who wears an armband to distinguish him- or herself from the rest of the players. The team captains have four responsibilities during a competitive game. Before the game begins, the captains meet the referees for a coin toss to determine which end of the field they'll defend and who will have possession of the ball for the opening pass. The captains are also in charge of executing player substitutions and identifying the goalie. If the captain is ever suspended or needs to be replaced, it is his or her duty to appoint a new captain. Finally, it is the captain's responsibility

This field hockey stadium was built specifically for the 1996 Olympics in Atlanta, Georgia. The playing field measures 100 yards by 60 yards (91 m by 55 m), or about the size of a professional football field.

7 Feet
or
2.13 Meters

12 Feet or 3.66 Meters

The goalie is responsible for defending the 7-by-12-foot (2.1 m by 3.7 m) goal area. Although goalies can use any part of their body to stop the ball, they have to use their stick when outside of the striking circle.

to make sure that his or her teammates behave properly, are respectful of the game's rules, and exhibit good sportsmanship.

In field hockey, there are two referees, one for each half of the field. The referees enforce the rules and make sure the game is played fairly. They are positioned on the sidelines and only enter the field when necessary. Each referee is responsible only for his or her half of the field and is in charge of calling violations on players, deciding when a ball is knocked out of bounds, and when to award a team with a penalty shot or a free hit.

The game is played in two halves, each half running between twenty-five and thirty-five minutes long, depending on the league, with a halftime break that lasts about ten minutes. Each half is played continuously, although sometimes two sixty-second time-outs are allotted to each team. After halftime, the teams change to the other side of the field and swap goals, so that there are no unfair advantages due to the makeup of the field. The beginning of each half of the game is started with a "passback" at the center of the field, after the referee has blown his or her whistle. A player must pass the ball to a team-mate who is at least 3.3 feet (1 m) back. Passbacks are also used after an opposing team has scored a goal.

Much like soccer players, field hockey players are not allowed to use their hands to touch the ball. The rules specify that players may only use their sticks when handling the ball, except for the goalie, who is permitted to use any part of his or her body to prevent a goal. The goalie is also allowed to kick the ball, but only when he or she is inside the striking circle. If a goalie is outside of the striking circle, the same stick-only rule applies to him or her as it does for the rest of the team.

The most common move in field hockey is a "drive." A drive is when a player applies a hard backswing to the ball, with both hands together at the top of the stick. It is used on passes and shots on the goal. A "scoop" is when the curve of the stick is used to scoop up the ball over an opponent's stick. A "push pass" is a quick stroke with the wrist and is considered the most accurate pass. A "slap shot" is the most powerful stroke in field hockey. It is a hard shot on the goal, executed with a half

SHELBYVILLE-SHELBY COUNTY
PUBLIC LIBRARY

backswing and hands slightly apart on the stick. The motions of many field hockey strokes are similar to that of a golf swing. However, when playing the ball in field hockey, raising the stick above the shoulder is considered a dangerous use of the stick, and a foul will be called.

A color-coded card system is used to distinguish the severity of an infraction or penalty. Green cards are issued by the referee as a warning for minor violations. Yellow cards are issued by the referee for an intentional foul, such as rough play. A player who receives a yellow card is suspended from the game for five minutes. The team must play one member short during that time. Red cards are issued for serious intentional fouls such as deliberate body contact or verbal abuse. A player who receives a red card is ejected from the game and will be suspended from the team's next game.

Fouls and rule violations are often committed and called on players for a number of reasons. An "obstruction" is called against a player who uses his or her stick, shoulder, or body as a barrier. While shielding the ball with one's body is part of the game strategy in most sports, it is not allowed in field hockey, where each player is supposed to have an equal chance at the ball as it is played up and down the field. Instead of using obstruction as a means to gain control of the ball, players are allowed to "jab," which means continual poking at the ball to make the opponent lose possession. "Back stick" is called when a player uses the round (back) side of the hockey stick to play the ball. "Undercutting" is called when a player chops at the ball with his or her stick, to lift it in an unsafe manner. "Hooking" is called when a player uses the curved head of his or her stick to hook an opponent's stick. "Advancing" is called when a player pushes or moves the ball in any way other than with his or her stick. When a foul is called on a player, a free hit from a penalty corner is awarded to the opposing team.

The Striking Circle

The striking circle is actually a semicircle that is shaped like the capital letter D. Because of its shape, the striking circle is also known as the D.

STRIKING CIRCLE

Most scoring opportunities in field hockey come from free hits and hits from penalty corners (also known as short corners). A free hit is awarded on any violation that takes place outside the striking circle and takes place at the location of the foul. All opposing players must stand at least 5 yards (4.6 m) away from where the hit is taken. Most free hits are taken as a drive, push pass, scoop, or flick. A hit from a penalty corner is awarded to the offense when the defensive team commits a foul inside the striking circle or intentionally hits the ball out of bounds. The penalty corner shot is taken from a point on the goal line, at least 10 yards (9.1 m) away from the goal. The rest of the offense must stand with their feet and sticks outside of the striking circle, while four defense players and their goalie stand behind the end line.

A penalty stroke is a little bit different from a hit from a penalty corner. A penalty stroke is awarded to the offense when a referee concludes that a defensive violation hampered a sure goal. An offensive player then goes one-on-one with the goalie and is given five seconds to shoot. All other players must remain behind the 25-yard (23 m) line. A 16-yard (15 m) hit is awarded to the defense when the offense sends the ball over the end line or commits a violation within the striking circle. The ball is placed 16 yards (15 m) from the spot of the violation or from where the ball went out of bounds.

This Dartmouth College player takes practice shots against her team's goalie. Field hockey, like any sport, requires that players practice a lot to keep in shape and improve their skills.

Although field hockey goals occur more frequently than goals in soccer, field hockey is generally a low-scoring game. If the game is tied, the teams may play ten minutes of sudden death overtime, depending on the level or league. Generally, a high school game will not go into overtime unless it is a championship game. For a non-championship game, a tie score is acceptable. During sudden death, there is a ten-minute game of "seven a side." This is when seven players from each team, six fielders and the goalie, play for ten minutes, with

During a sudden death overtime, the first team to score a goal wins the game. This goalie gets low to try and deflect a shot from the opposing team's center.

regular game rules applying. The first team to score during sudden death wins. If no team scores, there is a five-minute break, after which the teams return for another ten-minute seven-a-side game. If there is still no score made in this time, the game switches to penalty score mode. Each team chooses five strokers, so called because of the penalty stroke they execute. The strokers go up against the opposing goalie one at a time and take a shot on the goal, each team alternating goalies every other shot. The first team to score wins.

CHAPTER FOUR

Offense and Defense

The goalie can use any part of his or her body to deflect shots.

Often described as soccer with sticks, field hockey is played by two teams, each with eleven members on the field (ten players and one goalie). Two key aspects to team playing are communication and organization. Talking among teammates during a game is necessary for victory. Nonverbal communication is also important. Eye contact and head nods, for example, are important when passing the ball and indicating where the ball should go. A player should know and understand the full duties not only of his or her own position, but of every other player on the field. Only then can a player make the right decisions during a game.

Forwards are the main offensive players of the team. There are three forwards on the front line, two inside forwards, and two wings. The forwards' job is to invade the defense's area and score a goal. Most of their work is carried out in the 25-yard (23 m) area of the opposing team. Whenever the ball is in this area, the offense has a chance of scoring. All of their efforts are put toward getting the ball into the striking circle and positioning it for a goal.

The inside forwards stand in front of the goalie, positioning themselves to take a shot. They also try to block the goalie's view. The more they distract the goalie, the better the chances are for making a goal. The chief duty of the wings is to locate themselves in the zone in front of each goalpost. From this area, they can gain control of wide shots made on the goal, as well as following up on rebounds. Verbal communication is necessary in order for teammates to let each other know who has the best shot at the goal. When forwards feel like they have an opportunity to score they shout, "Stroke!" to let the other offensive linesmen know where they are, so the ball can be passed to them.

Midfielders have the difficult task of playing both defense and offense, and they are required to do a lot of running, as they are the only players that play all 50 yards (46 m) of the field. Midfielders are the offensive support for the forwards and need to stay close to the

striking circle when the front line is attacking. When the opposing team is on the attack, midfielders must quickly recede and help the backs during defense.

The backs are the main defensive unit of the team. One of the main duties of a back is to "mark up." Marking up is the most intense and important defense in field hockey. It is basically guarding the opposing forwards one on one. When the ball enters the 25-yard (23 m) defense area, every back must mark up the opponent's forward who is opposite them. Because forwards are constantly trying to obstruct a goalie's view and concentration, a back needs to try his or her hardest to defend the goalie.

The goalie and the sweeper are the last line of defense against the opposing team. They work together to guard the goal. The goalie and sweeper are the only defensive players who do not mark up, but because they are centrally located at the end of the field, they have the best view of the game playing out before them. This allows them to direct the rest of the defense, calling out the numbers of offensive players who are not being marked up and who pose a threat to the goal. A goalie's main duty is to block every shot, using every part of his or her body to do so as long as he or she is in the striking circle. The sweeper's duty is to cover any unguarded offensive player who moves in toward the cage. Because the sweeper is the last defender before the goal, he or she is often up against at least two unmarked offensive players working together to score on the goal. That is why it is crucial for

The players on this defensive squad prepare themselves for an attack by the opposing team. While defensive players might not get as much attention as the offense, the job they do is just as important.

Just because field hockey is a low-scoring game, it doesn't mean that it is an unexciting one. A good game of field hockey involves skill, strategy, and lots of action.

the sweeper and the goalie to have constant communication, so that the goalie will know what moves the sweeper plans on making and can judge where to place his or her body to best protect the goal.

Defense begins long before the offense has positioned the ball in the striking circle. Defensive playing should begin the moment the opposing team gains control of the ball. At that point, every player on the field, no matter what his or her position is, needs to think

Being a goalie is a hard job with a lot of pressure. The goalie spends a lot of time diving for the ball and fending off drives from the other team. Good goalkeeping can mean the difference between winning and losing.

defensively in order to protect the goal and to regain control of the ball. If players can't switch their thinking from offense to defense, they leave a weak spot for the opposing team to swoop in and score. Other than guarding the goal, the most important aspect of defensive playing is trying to recover the ball from the opposing team.

It is important for players to have a knowledge and understanding of the game beyond the physical requirements it takes to be great

field hockey players. It is primarily a game of skill, stamina, and strength, but a player who thinks strategically will be able to solve problems, defend the goal, and maintain control of the ball. A good diet and lots of exercise are also vital for a player to get the most out of his or her game. Being both mentally and physically prepared is the best defensive strategy of all. And like anything else, the only way to improve is to practice, practice, practice.

Field hockey continues to be embraced by more and more players around the world. Of the more than 200,000 people who play field hockey each year in the United States, 98 percent are students. Field hockey has become an important part of the extracurricular program in most high schools and colleges. Beginning in the early 1980s, the National Collegiate Athletic Association (NCAA) began holding field hockey tournaments among different schools to crown a champion. In the United States, schools in the Northeast have dominated the NCAA championships for the past twenty years. Perhaps this is because Northeastern schools have had field hockey programs since the sport was first introduced to America at the turn of the century by Constance Applebee. But within the past few years, schools from the West and Midwest have been proving to be worthy competitors, with the University of Michigan's women's field hockey team taking home the NCAA Division I National Championship in 2001.

The fact that teams who pose a threat to the championship title continue to pop up all over the country is a testament to the ever-

Players on the United States field hockey team congratulate each other after a key goal in a game against the Canadian team on August 7, 2003. Field hockey is popular all over the world, with competitions drawing thousands of fans.

Even if you don't become a professional player, getting involved in field hockey is a great way to stay in shape and meet new friends. Although it's nice to win, the most important thing about playing field hockey is having a good time.

growing popularity of the sport of field hockey. Today field hockey championships are played all over the world, with club championships, European championships, Asian games, Pan-American Games, and Inter-Continental Cup tournaments for qualification in the honored World Cup. The tournament for the most coveted international prize in hockey, the World Cup, is held every four years, with sixteen teams for men and sixteen teams for women competing for the title. The

Olympic Games are also held every four years, with the best of the best competing for their home country.

Because the game has such international appeal, the future of field hockey is promising, particularly for young American women. The NCAA currently has more than seventy-five Division I universities with active women's field hockey programs. Its popularity in the college circuit has managed to make field hockey a great source for college scholarship money.

The USFHA has set up a hall of fame based on the athletic achievement, long-term supremacy, innovation, and contributions to the sport for players and coaches in the United States. In order to qualify for the USFHA Hall of Fame, an individual must have been on his or her team for a minimum of five years. The USFHA Hall of Fame is located at Ursinus College in Pennsylvania.

GLOSSARY

advancing   To push or move the ball without using the stick.

Astroturf   A synthetic, grasslike playing surface.

backstick   To use the round, back side of the stick to play the ball.

defense   The team protecting the goal from the offense.

drive   To hit the ball with a hard backswing.

Dyneema   A man-made fiber that provides strength and absorption, yet is lightweight and flexible. It is used in making the field hockey stick.

hocquet   The French term for a shepard's crook, from which hockey is derived.

hook   The head shape of the stick that hooks up in order to provide the maximum surface area for receiving and hitting the ball.

jab   To use the stick to take the ball away from an opponent.

Kevlar   A man-made organic fiber that, like Dyneema, is used to strengthen the field hockey stick.

kilt   A pleated skirt traditionally worn by Scotsmen, which today is part of most women's field hockey uniforms.

kolbe   A German term for stick.

league   An association of teams that plays competitive sports.

midi   The head shape of the stick that is slightly longer than the shorti shape, with a larger hitting and stopping area.

offense   The attacking team; the team trying to score a goal.

opponent   A member of the opposite team.

passback   Passing the ball to a teammate behind you at the beginning of a game.

push pass   A quick stroke of the stick using the wrist that executes an accurate pass.

reinforcement   Something that strengthens.

scoop   To hit the ball over the opponent's stick.

shorti   The head shape of the stick carved from one piece of wood. This allows for quick maneuvering of the ball.

slapshot   A powerful shot on the goal, made by using the back swing with hands slightly apart.

suffrage   The right to vote.

undercutting   To chop at the ball with the stick, lifting it in an unsafe way.

FOR MORE INFORMATION

Organizations

Fédération Internationale de Hockey (FIH)
Avenue des Arts, 1 bte 5
1210 Bruxelles, Belgium
Web site: http://www.fihockey.org

Lead the Way, Inc.
P.O. Box 523
Saunderstown, RI 02874
Web site: http://www.leadthewayfieldhockey.com

National Collegiate Athletic Association (NCAA)
700 West Washington Street
P.O. Box 6222
Indianapolis, IN 46206
Web site: http://www.ncaa.org

National Federation of State High School Associations (NFHS)
P.O. Box 690
Indianapolis, IN 46206
Web site: http://www.nfhs.org

U.S. Field Hockey Association (USFHA)
One Olympic Plaza
Colorado Springs, CO 80909
Web site: http://www.usfieldhockey.com

Web Sites

Due to the changing nature of Internet links, the Rosen Publishing Group, Inc., has developed an online list of Web sites related to the subject of this book. This site is updated regularly. Please use this link to access the list:

http://www.rosenlinks.com/scc/fiho

FOR FURTHER READING

Anders, Elizabeth, and Sue Myers. *Field Hockey: Steps to Success.* Champaign, IL: Human Kinetics, 1998.

Martin, Wendy, and William F. Axton. *Field Hockey.* New York: McGraw Hill, 1993.

Marx, Josef, and Gunter Wagner. *Field Hockey Training for Young Players: Introducing the Game to Young Players.* Berlin: Meyer & Meyer Fachverlag und Buchhandel, 2000.

BIBLIOGRAPHY

Anders, Elizabeth, and Sue Myers. *Field Hockey: Steps to Success.* Champaign, IL: Human Kinetics, 1998.

Swissler, Becky, and Tracey Belbin. *Winning Field Hockey for Girls.* New York: Facts on File, 2003.

SHELBYVILLE-SHELBY COUNTY
PUBLIC LIBRARY

INDEX

About the Author

Helen Connolly is a freelance writer who lives in Brooklyn, New York.

Photo Credits

Cover images (field, team, goalie, and player on right), pp. 1 (right), 3, 6, 15, 16, 17, 20, 24, 30, 38 © Maura B. McConell; p. 1 © Timothy D. Easley/AP/World Wide Photos; p. 4 (top) © Nimatallah/Art Resource; p. 4 (bottom) © Lauros/Giraudon/Bridgeman Art Library; p. 8 © United States Field Hockey Association; p. 10 © Wally McNamee/ Corbis; pp. 12 (top), 35 © Thad Parsons/Icon Sports Media; p. 12 (bottom) © Max Nash/AP/World Wide Photos; pp. 14, 28 © Phil Schermeister/Corbis; p. 18 © Mike King/Corbis; pp. 22 (top), 24 (inset) © Nelson Sá; p. 22 (bottom) © Jon Bazemore/AP/World Wide Photos; p. 27 © Louisa Gouliamaki/AP/World Wide Photos; pp. 29, 36 © Silvia Izquierdo/AP/World Wide Photos; p. 32 © Bob Galbraith/ AP/World Wide Photos; p. 34 © Orban Thierry/Corbis.

Thanks to Westtown High School, Westtown, Pennsylvania.

Designer: Nelson Sá; **Editor**: Leigh Ann Cobb; **Photo Researcher:** Rebecca Anguin-Cohen